Exhale

WOMEN'S AFFIRMATION JOURNAL

Dr. Asha Fields Brewer

THIS JOURNAL BELONGS TO:

To the SHE Tea Community

Enjoy Books & Journals
by Dr. Asha

Eat, Drink, Do:
3 Basic Principles for Health by the Bible

Overflow:
6 Strategies to Beat Burnout
& Reclaim Your Abundant Life

Reflection:
Women's Wellness Journal

The collection is available at
www.doctorasha.com/books

Contents

Hi There,

I am so grateful that you picked up this journal, and I am excited for you. When we exhale, it is a sign of letting go. In fact, the synonym for exhale is to "expire". Exhaling is an opportunity to rid our bodies of what has expired in our lives—thoughts, habits, emotions, relationships, and more. Much like in our physical bodies, if this waste does not get expelled, it can cause us to suffocate.

Another word for inhale is to "inspire". This is so fitting because the very act of breathing is our most intimate connection to God. When we inhale, we invite God's Spirit to take up residence. We create space to be inspired by His love, joy, peace, patience, power, wisdom, and whatever else we need at that moment. When we inhale, we invite the healing presence of the Breath of Life.

As you breathe, I pray this journal helps you discover life abundantly. You will be led to exhale in six strategic areas: physical, spiritual, mental & emotional, intellectual, social, and career & financial. To learn more about these areas, I invite you to pick up *Overflow: Six Strategies to Beat Burnout & Reclaim Your Abundant Life* as a companion to this guided journal. Enjoy this time as you exhale.

Download Your Gift
www.doctorasha.com/links

Live Life Abundantly,

Dr. Asha

IT'S TIME TO

Exhale

Breathe

Before you start journaling, set aside a few moments to breathe. Close your eyes and breathe at your regular pace. Do this for several rounds of inhalation and exhalation.

[Breathe at Your Pace]

Next, extend your inhales by counting to five in your mind as you slowly take in each breath. Draw the breath in through your nose and imagine that it is gently inflating your stomach. At the deepest point of your inhale, pause, before transitioning to exhale. Do this for a few rounds of inhalation and exhalation.

[Inhale Slowly]

Following these rounds, start extending your exhalations as well. Count to five in your mind as you slowly release air from your mouth.

[Exhale Slowly]

Affirm

Now that you have slowed down your pace of breathing, you are ready to add your affirmation. Read your chosen affirmation aloud three times with focus and intention. Envision these words unfolding in your life. Experience them with your eyes, your ears, and your emotions. Bring this truth into your present moment.

[Read Affirmation Aloud, 3x]

Afterward, take a few deep breaths to savor the affirmation. The affirmations are inspired by the Bible, allowing the truth of God's Word to inhabit your most intimate spaces. It is this truth that ultimately leads to freedom.

The affirmations are brief, so you can easily tuck them into your heart's memory. When you're ready, consider closing your eyes or softly gazing at a point in front of you that doesn't move. Now, repeat the affirmation three more times from your heart.

[Repeat Affirmation, 3x]

Reflect

Once you have meditated on the affirmation several times, take a few moments to calmly return to your regular breathing rate. Open your eyes or shift your gaze only when you feel ready to do so.

Each affirmation comes with space to reflect afterward and record your thoughts. Reflect on what you have released into the atmosphere. Then envision and embrace what you have created space to receive. You may also choose to read the verses that inspired the affirmation and include these thoughts in your reflection. Use the prompt provided to get you started. If you run out of space to write in each section, it's not a problem. There are extra pages in the back of the journal to help you continue to explore.

[Complete Journal Prompt]

Practice Daily

You can practice deep breathing and meditation for five minutes, an hour, or however much time you allow. You can do this activity from anywhere—your desk, your parked car, the bathroom, etc. Once you have incorporated deep breathing into your routine, you may explore adding things like essential oils, nature sounds, or even different styles of deep breathing to modify your practice.

You may realize that pausing to breathe, affirm, and reflect does not change your circumstances, but it does change you. It changes your perspective; it shifts your focus; and it gives you room to exhale. I invite you to savor the words of your affirmation. Return to them throughout your day, your week, and your month. You may be inspired to write your own affirmations as well.

If you'd like personal guidance on developing your affirmation practice, head to www.doctorasha.com/links. Here, you can download the "Self-Care in 5 Minutes" handout and make this practice your own. I also invite you to listen to the "Affirmation of the Month" episodes on the *Good Health for Busy People*™ podcast, where I guide you to breathe, affirm, and reflect on God's truth.

Make it your life practice to pause on purpose. Release what no longer serves you and create space for what does. It's time to exhale.

Download Your Gift
www.doctorasha.com/links

SECTION ONE

Physical

The Physical Exhale

We will encounter days, even seasons, when the Physical Self just cannot keep up the pace on its own. When the Physical Self is overwhelmed to this extent, we become susceptible to diseases of the mind, body, and soul.[1] That is why we must regularly position ourselves for release. As your Physical Self exhales, consider what you create space for in this season and the seasons to come.

In this section, you will affirm…

Life Abundantly

Energy

Overflow

Rest

Good Health

---

[1] "Physical Self" (Adapted from p. 38, *Overflow: 6 Strategies to Beat Burnout & Reclaim Your Abundant Life* by A. Fields Brewer, 2020, AB Creations, LLC).

Life Abundantly

I breathe life.

I speak life.

I live life,
abundantly.

Inspired by Genesis 2:7, Proverbs 18:21, and John 10:10

Today's Date: _____/_____/_____

Use this space to reflect on what you release.

When I physically exhale...

Use this space to reflect on what you receive.

I create space for...

Energy

I run with God's energy.

He positions me to win.

I walk without fainting.

The Spirit sets my pace.

Inspired by Isaiah 40:31; Galatians 5:25; and Philippians 2:13, MSG

Today's Date: _____/_____/_____

Use this space to reflect on what you release.

When I physically exhale...

Use this space to reflect on what you receive.

I create space for...

Overflow

I refill before
I reach out.

I pause before I pour.

I refresh with
living water.

My cup overflows.

Inspired by John 4:10, 14 and Psalm 23:5

Today's Date: _____/_____/_____

Use this space to reflect on what you release.

When I physically exhale...

Use this space to reflect on what you receive.

I create space for...

Rest

I rest.

I rise.

I reflect.

I shine.

Inspired by Ephesians 5:14

Today's Date: _____/_____/_____

Use this space to reflect on what you release.

When I physically exhale...

Use this space to reflect on what you receive.

I create space for...

Good Health

I am prosperous.

I am in good health.

My soul is prosperous.

I am in good hands.

Inspired by 3 John 1:2

Today's Date: _____/_____/_____

Use this space to reflect on what you release.

When I physically exhale...

Use this space to reflect on what you receive.

I create space for...

SECTION TWO

Spiritual

The Spiritual Exhale

Despite everything we may experience and every anxiety we may face, we still have God on our side. Our side may not look like the winning side during the battle, circumstance, or distress. However, we are guaranteed that it will "work together for good" (Romans 8:28).[2] As your Spiritual Self exhales, consider what you create space for in this season and the journey to come.

In this section, you will affirm…

Security

Discovery

Salvation

Growth

Trust

---

[2] "Spiritual Self" (Adapted from p. 58, *Overflow: 6 Strategies to Beat Burnout & Reclaim Your Abundant Life* by A. Fields Brewer, 2020, AB Creations, LLC).

Security

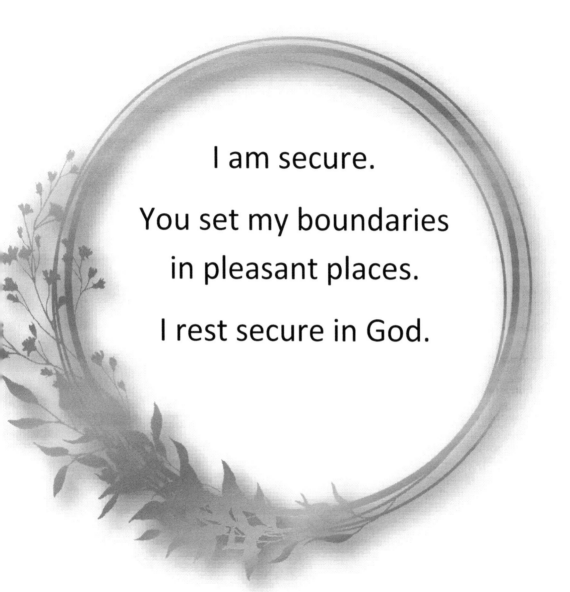

I am secure.

You set my boundaries
in pleasant places.

I rest secure in God.

Inspired by Psalm 16

Today's Date: _____/_____/_____

Use this space to reflect on what you release.

When I spiritually exhale...

Use this space to reflect on what you receive.

I create space for...

Discovery

I search my thoughts,
You are there.

I search my heart,
You are there.

I search my life,
You are there.

I discover myself
in You.

Inspired by Psalm 139:1-16, MSG

Today's Date: _____/_____/_____

Use this space to reflect on what you release.

When I spiritually exhale...

Use this space to reflect on what you receive.

I create space for...

Salvation

God sees me.

God hears me.

God delivers me.

I am saved.

Inspired by Psalm 34:15-17

Today's Date: _____/_____/_____

Use this space to reflect on what you release.

When I spiritually exhale...

Use this space to reflect on what you receive.

I create space for...

Growth

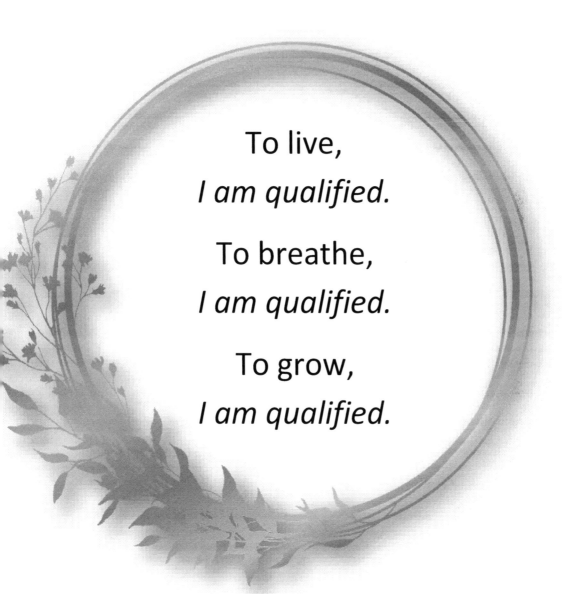

To live,
I am qualified.

To breathe,
I am qualified.

To grow,
I am qualified.

Inspired by Colossians 2:18-19

Today's Date: _____/_____/_____

Use this space to reflect on what you release.

When I spiritually exhale...

Use this space to reflect on what you receive.

I create space for...

Trust

I trust You, God.

I am patient for You.

I breathe Your Spirit.

I am patient for You.

Inspired by Proverbs 3:5-6 and Ephesians 4:30, MSG

Use this space to reflect on what you release.

When I spiritually exhale...

Use this space to reflect on what you receive.

I create space for...

SECTION THREE

Mental & Emotional

The Mental & Emotional Exhale

God wants us to feel authentically, so He invites us to experience a range of emotions. If we force happiness blinders on, we may deny ourselves the opportunity to heal through grief or sorrow. As such, we must learn how to properly process the emotions we are feeling. When these emotions are no longer serving to heal, mold, or mature us, then we should permit ourselves to release these emotions from our hearts.[3] As your Mental & Emotional Self exhales, consider what you create space for in this season and the journey to come.

In this section, you will affirm…

Release

Forgiveness

Your Testimony

Rejoicing

Peace

---

[3] "Mental & Emotional Self" (Adapted from p. 78, *Overflow: 6 Strategies to Beat Burnout & Reclaim Your Abundant Life* by A. Fields Brewer, 2020, AB Creations, LLC).

Release

I release pride.

I release expectations.

I release obligations.

I am free.

Inspired by John 8:36

Today's Date: _____/_____/_____

Use this space to reflect on what you release.

When I mentally & emotionally exhale...

Use this space to reflect on what you receive.

I create space for...

Forgiveness

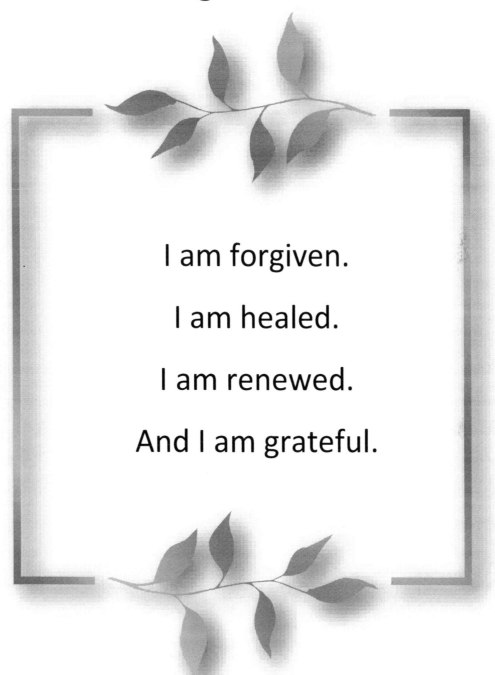

I am forgiven.

I am healed.

I am renewed.

And I am grateful.

Inspired by Psalm 103:1-5

Today's Date: _____/_____/_____

Use this space to reflect on what you release.

When I mentally & emotionally exhale...

Use this space to reflect on what you receive.

I create space for...

Testimony

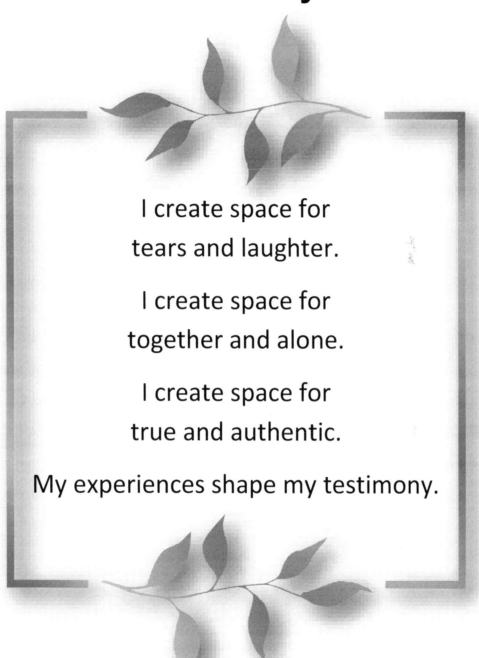

I create space for
tears and laughter.

I create space for
together and alone.

I create space for
true and authentic.

My experiences shape my testimony.

Inspired by Ecclesiastes 3:1-8

Today's Date: _____/_____/_____

Use this space to reflect on what you release.

When I mentally & emotionally exhale…

Use this space to reflect on what you receive.

I create space for…

Rejoicing

I rejoice in all seasons.

I am glad in my soul.

My reward is in Heaven.

It never runs out.

Inspired by Philippians 4:4 and Matthew 5:12

Today's Date: _____/_____/_____

Use this space to reflect on what you release.

When I mentally & emotionally exhale...

Use this space to reflect on what you receive.

I create space for...

Peace

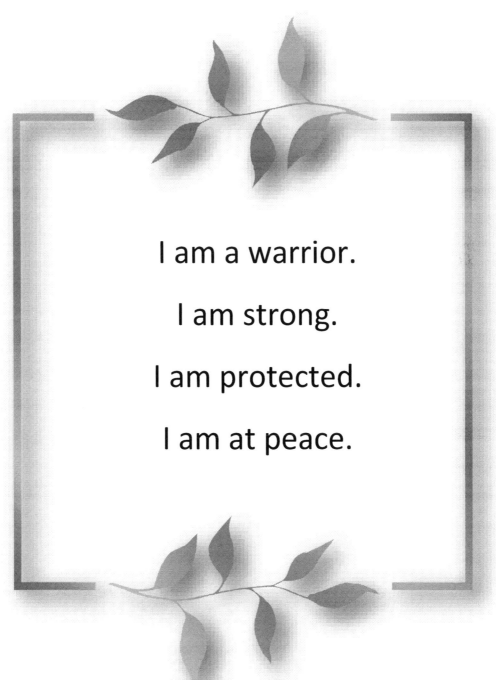

I am a warrior.

I am strong.

I am protected.

I am at peace.

Inspired by Ephesians 6:10-20

Today's Date: _____/_____/_____

Use this space to reflect on what you release.

When I mentally & emotionally exhale...

Use this space to reflect on what you receive.

I create space for...

SECTION FOUR

Intellectual

The Intellectual Exhale

When we are surrounded by pressure from work, family, society, and self, we easily lose sight of our passions. We also become more critical/judgmental of ourselves and are more apt to compare our work to the work of others. Therefore, we must invest in changing our minds—how we think and what we think—so we can be restored to our well place. [4] As your Intellectual Self exhales, consider what you create space for in this season and the journey to come.

In this section, you will affirm...

Memories

Motivation

Understanding

Help

Flow

---

[4] "Intellectual Self" (Adapted from pp. 86, 88, *Overflow: 6 Strategies to Beat Burnout & Reclaim Your Abundant Life* by A. Fields Brewer, 2020, AB Creations, LLC).

Memories

I remember Your patience.

I remember Your love.

I remember Your mercy.

I will not give up.

Inspired by Psalm 103:8-14

Today's Date: _____/_____/_____

Use this space to reflect on what you release.

When I intellectually exhale...

Use this space to reflect on what you receive.

I create space for...

Motivation

I evict
jealous thoughts.

I am motivated
from within.

In my Father's House
are many mansions.

There's room for
everyone to win.

Inspired by John 14:2, KJV

Today's Date: _____/_____/_____

Use this space to reflect on what you release.

When I intellectually exhale...

Use this space to reflect on what you receive.

I create space for...

Understanding

I seek wisdom;

I live long and well.

I seek understanding;

I live safe and secure.

Inspired by Proverbs 3:13-26, NIV

Today's Date: _____/_____/_____

Use this space to reflect on what you release.

When I intellectually exhale...

Use this space to reflect on what you receive.

I create space for...

Help

In wisdom,
I ask for help.

In humility,
I accept it.

Inspired by Ecclesiastes 4:9-12

Today's Date: _____/_____/_____

Use this space to reflect on what you release.

When I intellectually exhale...

Use this space to reflect on what you receive.

I create space for...

Flow

I embrace challenges,
I learn.

I embrace time,
I prepare.

I embrace focus,
I flow.

I am in perfect peace.

Inspired by Isaiah 26:3

Today's Date: _____/_____/_____

Use this space to reflect on what you release.

When I intellectually exhale...

Use this space to reflect on what you receive.

I create space for...

SECTION FIVE

Social

The Social Exhale

The greatest way to bring our social lives into abundance is to fill them with love. Love is for anyone who desires to have stimulating conversations, healthy relationships, and genuine connections throughout the life experience. That is why it is so important to know ourselves and how we love, so we can properly share and receive love from others.[5] As your Social Self exhales, consider what you create space for in this season and the journey to come.

In this section, you will affirm…

Friends

Love

Mentors

Family

Healthy Relationships

---

[5] "Social Self" (Adapted from p. 112, *Overflow: 6 Strategies to Beat Burnout & Reclaim Your Abundant Life* by A. Fields Brewer, 2020, AB Creations, LLC).

Friends

I am iron.

I attract *accountable* friends.

I attract *encouraging* friends.

I attract *honest* friends.

We sharpen each other.

Inspired by Proverbs 27

Today's Date: _____/_____/_____

Use this space to reflect on what you release.

When I socially exhale...

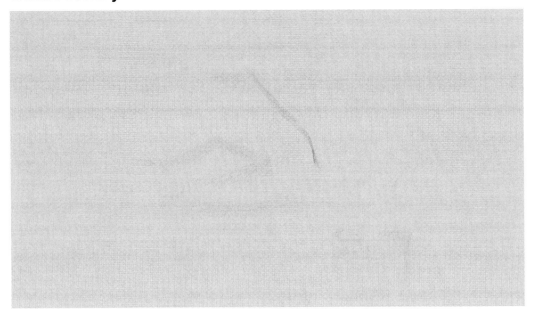

Use this space to reflect on what you receive.

I create space for...

Love

I am grounded
and stable.

I am grounded
and strong.

I am grounded
in love.

Inspired by Ephesians 3:14-19

Today's Date: _____/_____/_____

Use this space to reflect on what you release.

When I socially exhale...

Use this space to reflect on what you receive.

I create space for...

Mentors

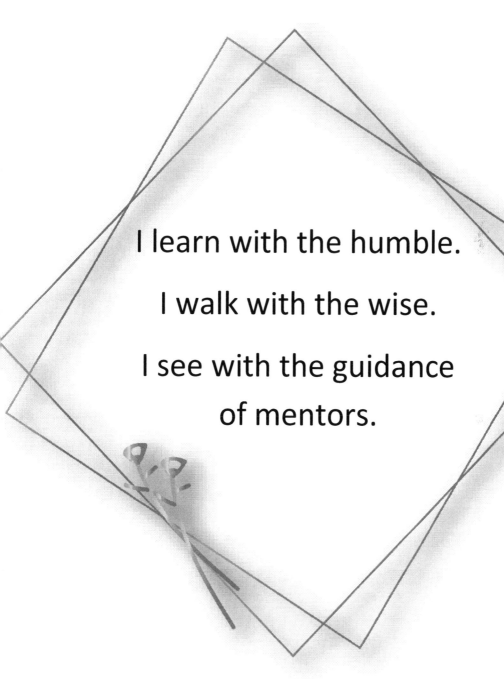

I learn with the humble.

I walk with the wise.

I see with the guidance
of mentors.

Inspired by Proverbs 13:20, Philippians 4:9

Today's Date: _____/_____/_____

Use this space to reflect on what you release.

When I socially exhale...

Use this space to reflect on what you receive.

I create space for...

Family

My roots
are in good soil;
God protects my seed.

My harvest
yields in season;
God protects my family.

Inspired by Mark 4:8

Today's Date: _____/_____/_____

Use this space to reflect on what you release.

When I socially exhale...

Use this space to reflect on what you receive.

I create space for...

Healthy Relationships

I *have*
healthy relationships.

I *have*
many reasons to smile.

I *have*
meaningful connections.

My life is full
of rewards.

Inspired by Ecclesiastes 4:9

Today's Date: _____/_____/_____

Use this space to reflect on what you release.

When I socially exhale...

Use this space to reflect on what you receive.

I create space for...

SECTION SIX

Career & Financial

The Career & Financial Exhale

"Do your best" is not synonymous with "be perfect." God graces us with the opportunity to do this work at this time and to pursue purpose in this way. Throughout the Bible, He reminds us that perfection is not the goal, purpose is. And it is in the places where we are imperfect that God's power shows up perfectly in our lives.[6] As your Career & Financial Self exhales, consider what you create space for in this season and the journey to come.

In this section, you will affirm…

Your Gift

Your Worth

Your Story

Your Purpose

Everything You Need

---

[6] "Career & Financial Self" (Adapted from p. 124-125, *Overflow: 6 Strategies to Beat Burnout & Reclaim Your Abundant Life* by A. Fields Brewer, 2020, AB Creations, LLC).

Gift

My work is beautiful.

My assignment is divine.

I grab the gift.

I release the grind.

Inspired by Ecclesiastes 3:9-13

Today's Date: _____/_____/_____

Use this space to reflect on what you release.

When I exhale in my career & finances...

Use this space to reflect on what you receive.

I create space for...

Worth

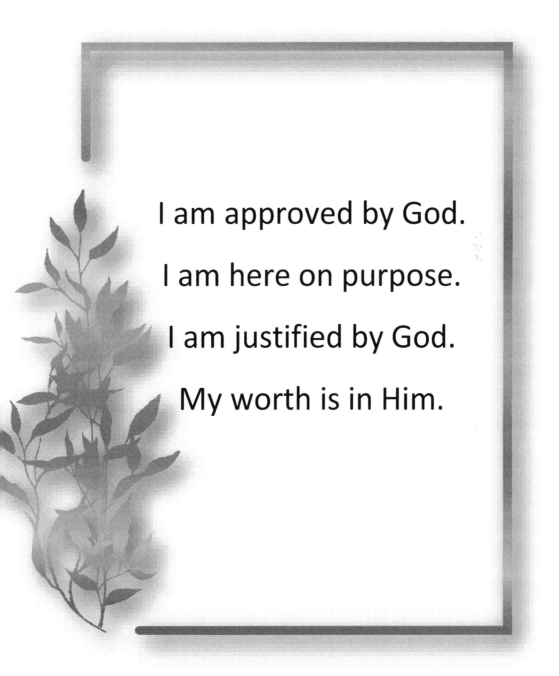

I am approved by God.

I am here on purpose.

I am justified by God.

My worth is in Him.

Inspired by Jeremiah 1:4-8, Romans 8:33

Today's Date: _____/_____/_____

Use this space to reflect on what you release.

When I exhale in my career & finances…

Use this space to reflect on what you receive.

I create space for…

Story

I hope
with an open heart.

I pray
with open ears.

I dream
with open eyes.

My story
makes sense to God.

Inspired by Jeremiah 29:10-14

Today's Date: _____/_____/_____

Use this space to reflect on what you release.

When I exhale in my career & finances...

Use this space to reflect on what you receive.

I create space for...

Purpose

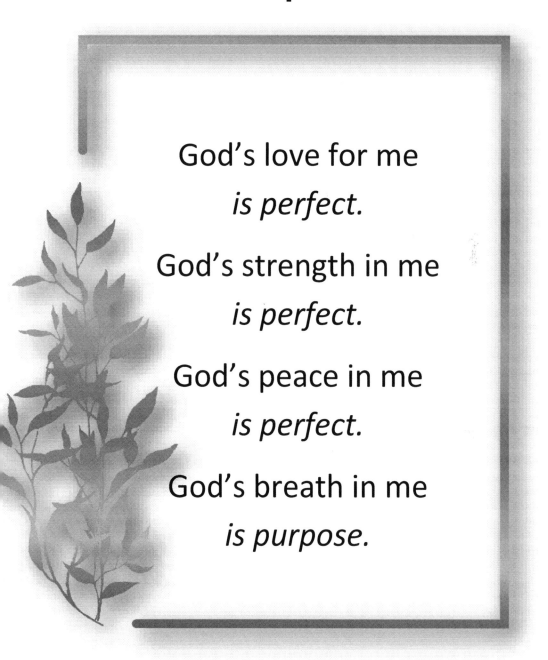

God's love for me
is perfect.

God's strength in me
is perfect.

God's peace in me
is perfect.

God's breath in me
is purpose.

Inspired by 1 John 4:16-19; 2 Corinthians 12:9-10; Isaiah 26:3; and Ephesians 4:30, MSG

Today's Date: _____/_____/_____

Use this space to reflect on what you release.

When I exhale in my career & finances...

Use this space to reflect on what you receive.

I create space for...

Everything

I have everything
I need,

To do everything
God wants.

Inspired by Psalm 23:1

Use this space to reflect on what you release.

When I exhale in my career & finances...

Use this space to reflect on what you receive.

I create space for...

WHEN I

Exhale...

When I Exhale...

When we are in uncertain situations, it is instinctive to hold our breath. Consider watching a suspenseful movie, rushing to meet a deadline, or waiting on a report from the doctor. All of our anticipations, anxieties, and fears gather in our chest like a block of cement. We turn inward to replay the "should'ves, could'ves, and would'ves" until we drive ourselves mad. All the while, our body, our whole being, is searching for a release.

This is what 2020 felt like for many people. Through the pandemic, social injustices, and a desperate economy—we held our breath. As a society, we struggled to manage our humanity. However, the one unifying force among all living creatures is the Breath of Life.[7] When God breathes His Spirit into us, we are intimately connected to Him. During this season, in particular, we were reminded not to take this gift for granted. [8]

Through inhalation, God gives you what you need to live: oxygen, inspiration, and hope. He refills you with His purpose. If you desire to breathe Him in more deeply, you must stop holding your breath. You must exhale to release toxins like carbon dioxide, distress, and burnout. You must exhale to evict harmful waste from your environment. You must exhale to assert your authority, reclaim your dominion over the earth, and shift the atmosphere. Ultimately, when you exhale, you embrace the power of letting go.

What else happens when you exhale? The remainder of this journal is for you to explore.

---

[7] Genesis 2:7
[8] Ephesians 4:30, MSG

Today's Date: _____/_____/_____

When I exhale…

_____

_____

_____

_____

_____

_____

_____

_____

_____

_____

_____

_____

_____

_____

_____

_____

_____

_____

_____

_____

_____

_____

_____

Today's Date: _____/_____/_____

When I exhale…

_____

_____

_____

_____

_____

_____

_____

_____

_____

_____

_____

_____

_____

_____

_____

_____

_____

_____

_____

_____

_____

_____

Today's Date: _____/_____/_____

When I exhale…

_____

_____

_____

_____

_____

_____

_____

_____

_____

_____

_____

_____

_____

_____

_____

_____

_____

_____

_____

_____

_____

_____

_____

Today's Date: _____/_____/_____

When I exhale…

_____

_____

_____

_____

_____

_____

_____

_____

_____

_____

_____

_____

_____

_____

_____

_____

_____

_____

_____

_____

_____

Today's Date: _____/_____/_____

When I exhale…

_____

_____

_____

_____

_____

_____

_____

_____

_____

_____

_____

_____

_____

_____

_____

_____

_____

_____

_____

_____

Today's Date: _____/_____/_____

When I exhale…

_____

_____

_____

_____

_____

_____

_____

_____

_____

_____

_____

_____

_____

_____

_____

_____

_____

_____

_____

_____

_____

_____

_____

_____

_____

Today's Date: _____/_____/_____

When I exhale…

_____

_____

_____

_____

_____

_____

_____

_____

_____

_____

_____

_____

_____

_____

_____

_____

_____

_____

_____

_____

_____

_____

_____

Today's Date: _____/_____/_____

When I exhale…

_____

_____

_____

_____

_____

_____

_____

_____

_____

_____

_____

_____

_____

_____

_____

_____

_____

_____

_____

_____

Today's Date: _____/_____/_____

When I exhale…

_____

_____

_____

_____

_____

_____

_____

_____

_____

_____

_____

_____

_____

_____

_____

_____

_____

_____

_____

_____

Today's Date: _____/_____/_____

When I exhale…

_____

_____

_____

_____

_____

_____

_____

_____

_____

_____

_____

_____

_____

_____

_____

_____

_____

_____

_____

_____

_____

Today's Date: _____/_____/_____

When I exhale…

_____

_____

_____

_____

_____

_____

_____

_____

_____

_____

_____

_____

_____

_____

_____

_____

_____

_____

_____

_____

Today's Date: _____/_____/_____

When I exhale…

_____

_____

_____

_____

_____

_____

_____

_____

_____

_____

_____

_____

_____

_____

_____

_____

_____

_____

_____

_____

_____

_____

Today's Date: _____/_____/_____

When I exhale…

_____

_____

_____

_____

_____

_____

_____

_____

_____

_____

_____

_____

_____

_____

_____

_____

_____

_____

_____

_____

_____

Today's Date: _____/_____/_____

When I exhale…

_____

_____

_____

_____

_____

_____

_____

_____

_____

_____

_____

_____

_____

_____

_____

_____

_____

_____

_____

_____

Today's Date: _____/_____/_____

When I exhale…

_____

_____

_____

_____

_____

_____

_____

_____

_____

_____

_____

_____

_____

_____

_____

_____

_____

_____

_____

_____

_____

_____

Today's Date: _____/_____/_____

When I exhale…

_____

_____

_____

_____

_____

_____

_____

_____

_____

_____

_____

_____

_____

_____

_____

_____

_____

_____

_____

_____

_____

Today's Date: _____/_____/_____

When I exhale…

_____

_____

_____

_____

_____

_____

_____

_____

_____

_____

_____

_____

_____

_____

_____

_____

_____

_____

_____

_____

_____

_____

Today's Date: _____/_____/_____

When I exhale…

Today's Date: _____/_____/_____

When I exhale…

_____

_____

_____

_____

_____

_____

_____

_____

_____

_____

_____

_____

_____

_____

_____

_____

_____

_____

_____

_____

_____

Today's Date: _____/_____/_____

When I exhale…

_____

_____

_____

_____

_____

_____

_____

_____

_____

_____

_____

_____

_____

_____

_____

_____

_____

_____

_____

_____

_____

Acknowledgments

This journal was designed to commemorate the 7th Annual SHE Tea: Women's Wellness Conference. This program is hosted by Temple Fit Health, Inc., 501 (c)(3), a faith-based wellness nonprofit organization. The conference provides a sacred space to have real conversations with real women about real life.

As we prepared for the 2020 conference, God gave me the theme of "Exhale" for the 2021 experience. In many ways, along with society, I have been holding my breath as we come to terms with injustice, disparities, grief, anxiety, and death. I am grateful for the continued inspiration, fellowship, and community that is SHE Tea. By God's grace, we empower each other to truly live life abundantly.

About the Author

Dr. Asha is a "Creator of Healthy Conversations."
As a national speaker, author, and radio host, she frequently contributes her insight to magazines, newspapers, and other media outlets. She earned a B.S. in Exercise Science from Florida State University and a Doctor of Chiropractic degree from Parker University. She founded the Temple Fit Co. wellness agency, and she empowers audiences alongside their 25+ wellness faculty. In everything she does, Dr. Asha is dedicated to her life purpose: teach the busy and overwhelmed how to live life abundantly. For more information and booking, visit www.doctorasha.com.

Contact the Author
For speaking engagements, book clubs, and workshops,
contact Dr. Asha's Team at
hello@doctorasha.com
www.doctorasha.com/speaking

Connect on Social Media
Facebook page: "Dr. Asha"
Instagram: @doctorasha

Download Your Gift
www.doctorasha.com/links

Made in United States
Orlando, FL
30 May 2022